CBT – DBT

Christian Companion

Mindfulness and Scripture

Linda Houts, MSW, LCSW

CBT – DBT
Christian Companion

This publication is designed to provide supportive information concerning the subject matter covered for educational purposes. It is sold with the understanding that the publisher is not engaged in rendering professional service. If you have questions or concerns about your emotional, medical, or religious well-being, seek expert assistance of a competent mental health, medical professional or clergy.

The views expressed in this work are solely those of the author. Reproduction for client use is authorized. Any other reproduction in any form is prohibited without the express written permission of the author.

Distributed by Amazon Kindle Direct Publishing

Copyright © 2022 by Linda Houts.

All Rights Reserved.

ISBN: 9798798073085
Imprint: Independently published

Contents

Core Mindfulness Christian Perspective	2
A	7
Abstinence	8
Acceptance	11
Anger	20
Applaud	25
B	27
Behavior Modification	28
C	31
Calm	32
Commitment to Change	37
Compassion	54
Crisis Survival	62
Compromise	83
D	87
Dialectics	88
Decrease Vulnerability	93
Distress Tolerance	94
E	98
Effectively	99
Embrace Change	104
Emotion Mind	105
Emotional Regulation	107
F	111
FAST	112
Fear	125
G	133
GIVE	134
Guilt	142
H	148

Hope	149
I	150
Interpersonal Effectiveness	157
J	158
Joy	159
L	162
Lighten Your Load	163
Letting Go	164
Loving Kindness	166
M	168
Making Repairs	169
Meditate	170
Mindfulness	171
N	182
Nonjudgmental Stance	183
O	190
One-mindfully	191
P	192
Pain	193
Present Moment Mindfulness	194
R	195
Reasonable Mind	196
Rest	197
S	198
Self-Care	199
Sooth the Moment	200
Self-Regulation	203

Core Mindfulness Christian Perspective

In applying Christian virtues of discernment, remembrance, and watchfulness, to mindfulness consider that we are encouraged to discern right thought and right action as a basic daily Christian practice. This is mindfulness.

The focus of core mindfulness skills are to develop awareness and insight in order to help us attain well-being. In Dialectical Behavioral Therapy (DBT) there are of two basic types 'what' and 'how' skills. 'What' to do to take control of your mind and 'how' to do it more effectively. What skills include observe, describe, and participate. How skills include non-Judgmentally, one-Mindfully, and effectively.

Consider the Christian virtues of watchfulness, discernment and remembrance in light of these DBT what and how skill definitions.

Watchfulness is the conscious attentive awareness and vigilance towards one's thoughts and emotions with mindfulness of Biblical truth, spiritual maturity and steadfastness.

Discernment is the spiritual gift of the ability, through thoughtful examination, to determine what is from God and what is not.

Right thought, right action, while, remembrance is to keep the mind focused upon God, the eternal and heavenly.

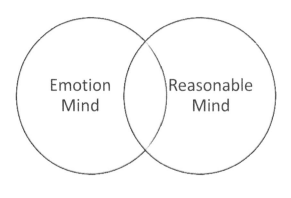

∧

Emotion Mind	Wise Mind	Reasonable Mind
Watchful conscious attentiveness towards one's emotions	Deliberate remembrance and discernment of Biblical truth and wisdom in spiritual maturity and peace, and steadfast effort in the present moment.	Watchful conscious attentiveness towards one's thoughts

Wise Mind is a wisdom process which helps us skillfully balance our thoughts, emotions and consequences.

In support please consider:

Philippians 2:5 NLV

Think as Christ Jesus thought.

Philippians 4:8 NLV

Christian brothers, keep your minds thinking about whatever is true, whatever is respected, whatever is right, whatever is pure, whatever can be loved, and whatever is well thought of. If there is anything good and worth giving thanks for, think about these things.

Philippians 4:9 NKJV

The things which you learned and received and heard and saw in me, these do, and the God of peace will be with you.

2 Corinthians 10:5 NLV

We break down every thought and proud thing that puts itself up against the wisdom of God. We take hold of every thought and make it obey Christ.

Romans 12:2 NLV

Do not act like the sinful people of the world. Let God change your life. First of all, let Him give you a new mind. Then you will know what God wants you to do. And the things you do will be good and pleasing and perfect.

12:2 NKJV

And do not be conformed to this world, but be transformed by the renewing of your mind, that you may prove what is that good and acceptable and perfect will of God. Romans

Matthew 6:34 NLV

Do not worry about tomorrow. Tomorrow will have its own worries. The troubles we have in a day are enough for one day.

Ecclesiastes 10:10 ESV

If the iron is blunt, and one does not sharpen the edge, he must use more strength, but wisdom helps one to succeed.

John 10:14 NLV

I am the Good Shepherd. I know My sheep and My sheep know Me.

A

Abstinence

Skill: Dialectic Abstinence

Dialectical abstinence embraces the concept of abstinence while acknowledging that people are imperfect humans. This acceptance and expectation of human imperfection allows us to acknowledge and normalize that anytime we are seeking to change a problem pattern we will, at times, revert to a previous pattern. Practice dialectic abstinence this by setting a goal to live today, or this hour or minute if you need to, without a problem behavior or substance while openly acknowledging the challenges and areas of risk specific to you and your situation. It is important to recognize that patterns, temptation, unwillingness, cravings, intense emotions and relational issues are normal parts of behavior change, as is relapse. When a relapse occurs, remember to keep it in perspective and proportion. Do not catastrophize. Use the experience as an opportunity to be curious and learn about yourself and circumstance, while at the same time reaffirming, and fully recommitting, to abstinence from the problem behavior or substance. Be sure to unpack any shame, or guilt, and seek reconciliation and forgiveness in Christ. Remember that it is the balance of acceptance and change that leads to recovery.

Abstinence

Dialectic Abstinence is the total avoidance when it is too dangerous to use middle ground.

Verse: Colossians 3:5-10 ESV

Put to death therefore what is earthly in you: sexual immorality, impurity, passion, evil desire, and covetousness, which is idolatry. On account of these the wrath of God is coming. In these you too once walked, when you were living in them. But now you must put them all away: anger, wrath, malice, slander, and obscene talk from your mouth. Do not lie to one another, seeing that you have put off the old self with its practices...

Suggested Common Language Meaning

These verses provide guidance for Christians to not participate or practice behaviors that trap a person in sin, and therefore, in suffering. Instead it is encouragement to strive to live a Christ-like life. Do not go in anger, outrage, evil intent or desire, do not lie or damage the reputation of another, and do not engage in sexual, lascivious or curse or wish ill upon another. Unspoken but, inferred in this verse is what behaviors are encouraged. Strive to be calm and even-tempered, let slights pass without response, speak only thing s you know to be true and just, and mind your language. By extension it is reasonable to conclude that 'evil desire' reference in this verse also suggests dialectic abstinence in any behavior that traps a person such as unhealthy drug use, alcohol use, self-injury behaviors, abuses of self or others.

*Notes:*_____
_____
_____
_____
_____
_____
_____
_____
_____
_____
_____

Acceptance

Acceptance is willingness to tolerate and endure the uncomfortable.

Proverbs 14:8-9 ESV

The wisdom of the prudent is to discern his way, but the folly of fools is deceiving.
Fools mock at the guilt offering, but the upright enjoy acceptance.

Suggested Common Language Meaning

Wisdom is demonstrating and acting with thoughtful consideration or discernment. The loss of an unwise or imprudent person is to believe something that is untrue or use deceit for personal gain. It is unwise to tease, mock or ridicule a person for making amends for sin, because the honorable and honest people are friendly, helpful, and cooperative.

*Notes:*_____
_____
_____
_____

Acceptance

Acceptance is willingness to tolerate and endure the uncomfortable (Houts, 2020).

1 Timothy 1:14-16 ESV

And the grace of our Lord overflowed for me with the faith and love that are in Christ Jesus. The saying is trustworthy and deserving of full acceptance, that Christ Jesus came into the world to save sinners, of whom I am the foremost. But I received mercy for this reason, that in me, as the foremost, Jesus Christ might display his perfect patience as an example to those who were to believe in him for eternal life.

Suggested Common Language Meaning

This verse speaks of Christ as a source of peace, love and mercy to his believers with acceptance and patience. The same acceptance, patience, peace, love and mercy we are to practice giving ourselves and others.

*Notes:*_____

_____

_____

_____

Acceptance

Acceptance is willingness to tolerate and endure the uncomfortable (Houts, 2020).

Psalm 46:10 NKJV

Be still, and know that I am God; I will be exalted among the nations, I will be exalted in the earth!

Suggested Common Language Meaning

God is our refuge in troubled times accept this and lean upon him for peace.

*Notes:*_____
_____
_____
_____
_____
_____
_____
_____

Acceptance

Acceptance is willingness to tolerate and endure the uncomfortable (Houts, 2020).

Jeremiah 29:11 NKJV

For I know the thoughts that I think toward you, says the Lord, thoughts of peace and not of evil, to give you a future and a hope.

Suggested Common Language Meaning

This verse reflects the unchanging nature of the Lord and his grace and affection for those he loves. Know that the Lord wishes you peace. Peace in troubled times requires acceptance of this fundamental nature of the Lord towards his followers.

*Notes:*_____
_____
_____
_____
_____
_____
_____

Acceptance

Acceptance is willingness to tolerate and endure the uncomfortable (Houts, 2020).

Ecclesiastes 3:1-5 NKJV

To everything there is a season,
A time for every purpose under heaven:
A time to be born, and a time to die;
A time to plant, and a time to pluck what is planted;
A time to kill, and a time to heal;
A time to break down, and a time to build up;
A time to weep, and a time to laugh;
A time to mourn, and a time to dance;
A time to cast away stones, and a time to gather stones;
A time to embrace, and a time to refrain from embracing;

Suggested Common Language Meaning

God has appointed the cycles of life. All of life is a cycle by design. We must be patient with the nature of life and accept the timing of all things.

Notes:_____
_____

Acceptance

Acceptance is willingness to tolerate and endure the uncomfortable (Houts, 2020).

Romans 15:5-7 NIV

May the God who gives endurance and encouragement give you the same attitude of mind toward each other that Christ Jesus had, so that with one mind and one voice you may glorify the God and Father of our Lord Jesus Christ. Accept one another, then, just as Christ accepted you, in order to bring praise to God.

Suggested Common Language Meaning

To bring glory to God we should be in acceptance of others with a good attitude, fortitude and encouragement, as Christ has accepted us.

*Notes:*_____
_____
_____
_____
_____
_____
_____

Acceptance

Acceptance is willingness to tolerate and endure the uncomfortable (Houts, 2020).

James 4:12 ESV

There is only one lawgiver and judge, he who is able to save and to destroy. But who are you to judge your neighbor?

Suggested Common Language Meaning

Judging is not our job. That privilege resides with God alone. Nonjudgmental stance is a basis of a Christian life according to this verse.

*Notes:*_____
_____
_____
_____
_____
_____ ___
_____
_____

Acceptance

Acceptance is willingness to tolerate and endure the uncomfortable (Houts, 2020).

Matthew 7:1 NKJV

Judge not, that you be not judged. For with what judgment you judge, you will be judged; and with the measure you use, it will be measured back to you.

Suggested Common Language Meaning

Do not condemn or punish others. This verse is about the hazards of evaluating others out of context. Consider primary attribution error. Primary attribution error states that when I make a decision I understand its complete context and it makes sense but when I look at the decisions of others, which I do not agree with, I conclude it is because of poor character. It is not our responsibility or privilege to condemn or punish because we cannot possibly understand the context.

*Notes:*_____
_____
_____
_____

Anger

Anger: Small Intensity: annoyance, displeasure, irritation. Medium intensity: aggravation, temper, ire. High intensity: anger, fury, rage. (Houts, 2020).

Proverbs 14:17 NIV

A quick-tempered person does foolish things, and the one who devises evil schemes is hated.

Suggested Common Language Meaning

Acting on the impulse of anger leads us to make rash, unwise and problematic actions, words and decisions. Evil schemes are contrary to the teachings of Crist, to feeling well, to having good relationships and living in the love and kindness that we have been instructed.

*Notes:*_____
_____
_____
_____
_____
_____ ____
_____

Anger

Anger: Small Intensity: annoyance, displeasure, irritation. Medium intensity: aggravation, temper, ire. High intensity: anger, fury, rage. (Houts, 2020).

Proverbs 14:29 NIV

Whoever is patient has great understanding, but one who is quick-tempered displays folly.

Suggested Common Language Meaning

One who remains calm and is slow to anger demonstrates understanding, and therefore wisdom. As opposed to being quick tempered, fault finding, of poor judgment and unwise.

*Notes:*_____
_____
_____
_____
_____
_____
_____
_____
_____

Anger

Anger: Small Intensity: annoyance, displeasure, irritation. Medium intensity: aggravation, temper, ire. High intensity: anger, fury, rage. (Houts, 2020).

Ephesians 4:26 ESV

Be angry and do not sin; do not let the sun go down on your anger.

Suggested Common Language Meaning

Anger is a normal human emotion and appropriate to give strength in appropriate circumstances, but do not get stuck there. Accept or change. Anger can be an effective tool in motivation to change that which we cannot continue to live with. But, be judicious in your anger. Simmering in anger with that which is normal everyday inconveniences, normal behaviors of others, using anger to attempt to control or using anger to mask other emotions leads us to regrettable thought patterns and behaviors.

Notes:_____
_____
_____

Anger

Anger: Small Intensity: annoyance, displeasure, irritation. Medium intensity: aggravation, temper, ire. High intensity: anger, fury, rage. (Houts, 2020).

Proverbs 29:22 ESV

A man of wrath stirs up strife, and one given to anger causes much transgression.

Suggested Common Language Meaning

Anger as a way of being causes him or herself to live a life of bitterness and difficulty as living and practicing anger inevitably leads to impulsive decisions and words. Impulsive decisions and words leads to making more problems in life.

*Notes:*_____
_____
_____
_____
_____
_____
_____ ___
_____

Anger

Anger: Small Intensity: annoyance, displeasure, irritation. Medium intensity: aggravation, temper, ire. High intensity: anger, fury, rage (Houts, 2020).

Proverbs 12:16 ESV

The vexation of a fool is known at once, but the prudent ignores an insult.

Suggested Common Language Meaning

The annoyance, frustration or worry of an unwise person is immediately apparent, but a wise person is able to act with self-control and choose not to be sucked in by the behaviors or words of others.

*Notes:*_____
_____
_____
_____
_____
_____
_____
_____

Applaud Yourself and Play Your Part

Cheer yourself for your efforts, count your wins and progress, play your part and do your share towards your goal.

Ephesians 4: 11-16

Christ gave gifts to men. He gave to some the gift to be missionaries, some to be preachers, others to be preachers who go from town to town. He gave others the gift to be church leaders and teachers. These gifts help His people work well for Him. And then the church which is the body of Christ will be made strong. All of us are to be as one in the faith and in knowing the Son of God. We are to be full-grown Christians standing as high and complete as Christ is Himself. Then we will not be as children any longer. Children are like boats thrown up and down on big waves. They are blown with the wind. False teaching is like the wind. False teachers try everything possible to make people believe a lie, but we are to hold to the truth with love in our hearts. We are to grow up and be more like Christ. He is the leader of the church. Christ has put each part of the church in its right place. Each part helps other parts. This is what is needed to keep the whole body together. In this way, the whole body grows strong in love.

Suggested Common Language Meaning

We are each born with special gifts needed at this place and time. These gifts are blessings which help us grow to be of service to God and our fellow man. Do not judge that some gifts are more important than others because this is not so. All parts of the body of Christ are needed to be whole. Do not fall for the tricks of the ego. Do not be rash, petty, act in anger and impulse. Hold yourself steady in the knowledge that our existence matters and our gifts matter. Know with deep wisdom that you are in the right place, at the right time, to do what you came to this Earthly life experience to do. Be strong in belief, strong in this fact, in loving kindness, in assistance to others, in acceptance of the assistance of others.

*Notes:*_____
_____
_____
_____
_____
_____ ___
_____
_____

B

Behavior Modification

Change your behavior.

1 Peter 2:12

When you are around people who do not know God, be careful how you act. Even if they talk against you as wrong-doers, in the end they will give thanks to God for your good works when Christ comes again.

Suggested Common Language Meaning

Be mindful of your behavior and conduct yourself in an upstanding way. Regardless, of the behavior of others. Your behaviors will speak for themselves and are a credit to you.

Notes:_____
_____
_____
_____
_____

Behavior Modification

Change your behavior.

Matthew 5:16 NKJV

Let your light so shine before men, that they may see your good works and glorify your Father in heaven.

Suggested Common Language Meaning

Be your best self so that others might see you inner light and fruit of the spirit, and come to know God through you.

Notes:_____
_____
_____
_____
_____
_____
_____
_____

Behavior Modification

Change your behavior.

2 Peter 1:5-8 NKJV

But also for this very reason, giving all diligence, add to your faith virtue, to virtue knowledge, to knowledge self-control, to self-control perseverance, to perseverance godliness, to godliness brotherly kindness, and to brotherly kindness love. For if these things are yours and abound, you will be neither barren nor unfruitful in the knowledge of our Lord Jesus Christ.

Suggested Common Language Meaning

Fruitful growth and blessings come from diligence, integrity, honor, self-control and perseverance, religiously devotion, kindness and unconditionally love. If you will practice these things you will be blessed with wisdom.

*Notes:*_____
_____
_____
_____

C

Calm

Calm: Small Intensity: cool, mild, serene. Medium intensity: tranquil, at peace, calm. High intensity: placid, imperturbable, sedate (Houts, 2020).

Proverbs 14:30 NKJV

A sound heart is life to the body, but envy is rottenness to the bones.

Suggested Common Language Meaning

To be in healthy emotional condition, in which emotions are in equilibrium. Envy, being jealous and resentful, will damage your foundation making it difficult to be upright.

*Notes:*_____
_____
_____
_____
_____
_____
_____

Calm

Calm: Small Intensity: cool, mild, serene. Medium intensity: tranquil, at peace, calm. High intensity: placid, imperturbable, sedate (Houts, 2020).

Philippians 4:6 ESV

Do not be anxious about anything, but in everything by prayer and supplication with thanksgiving let your requests be made known to God.

Suggested Common Language Meaning

Do not be anxious, pray with gratitude.

*Notes:*_____

_____

_____

_____

_____

_____

_____

_____

Calm

Calm: Small Intensity: cool, mild, serene. Medium intensity: tranquil, at peace, calm. High intensity: placid, imperturbable, sedate (Houts, 2020).

1 Corinthians 13:4-5 ESV

Love is patient and kind; love does not envy or boast; it is not arrogant or rude. It does not insist on its own way; it is not irritable or resentful;

Suggested Common Language Meaning

Love is accepting and gentle; love is not covetous, demanding, controlling, and believing one is superior to another. It does not dominate others. It is not angry or bitter or counting of transgressions or lack.

*Notes:*_____

_____

_____

_____

_____

_____

Calm

Calm: Small Intensity: cool, mild, serene. Medium intensity: tranquil, at peace, calm. High intensity: placid, imperturbable, sedate (Houts, 2020).

Acts 2:25 NLV

David said this about Him, 'I can see the Lord before me all the time. He is at my right side so that I do not need to be troubled.'

Suggested Common Language Meaning

The Lord walks with me. I need not be troubled.

*Notes:*_____
_____
_____
_____
_____
_____
_____
_____

Calm

Calm: Small Intensity: cool, mild, serene. Medium intensity: tranquil, at peace, calm. High intensity: placid, imperturbable, sedate (Houts, 2020).

John 16:33 NIV

"I have told you these things, so that in me you may have peace. In this world you will have trouble. But take heart! I have overcome the world."

Suggested Common Language Meaning

Be at peace. The Lord is in control. I am bigger than any worldly problem.

*Notes:*_____
_____
_____
_____
_____
_____
_____

Commitment to Change

An agreement or pledge to dedicate oneself to a new course or effort. All skill development requires commitment to change.

2 Timothy 1:7 ESV

For God gave us a spirit not of fear but of power and love and self-control.

Suggested Common Language Meaning

The nonphysical part of being human is of power, love and self-control.

*Notes:*_____

_____
_____
_____
_____
_____
_____
_____

Commitment to Change

An agreement or pledge to dedicate oneself to a new course or effort. All skill development requires commitment to change.

2 Corinthians 5:17 ESV

Therefore, if anyone is in Christ, he is a new creation. The old has passed away; behold, the new has come.

Suggested Common Language Meaning

In Christ we become new. Yesterday is gone, see the new in yourself today.

*Notes:*_____
_____
_____
_____
_____
_____
_____

Commitment to Change

An agreement or pledge to dedicate oneself to a new course or effort. All skill development requires commitment to change.

James 1:2-4 ESV

Count it all joy, my brothers, when you meet trials of various kinds, for you know that the testing of your faith produces steadfastness. And let steadfastness have its full effect, that you may be perfect and complete, lacking in nothing.

Suggested Common Language Meaning

Difficult times produce growth for us and lead us to our growth and completeness. Take joy in your challenges they are a normal, necessary, part of life's processes.

*Notes:*_____
_____
_____
_____

Commitment to Change

Commitment to change is an agreement or pledge to dedicate oneself to a new course or effort. All skill development requires commitment to change.

Mark 9:23 ESV

And Jesus said to him, "'If you can! All things are possible for one who believes."

Suggested Common Language Meaning

Jesus is able and willing to assist us if we can believe.

*Notes:*_____

_____
_____
_____
_____
_____
_____
_____

Commitment to Change

Commitment to change is an agreement or pledge to dedicate oneself to a new course or effort. All skill development requires commitment to change.

Deuteronomy 31:6 NKJV

Be strong and of good courage, do not fear nor be afraid of them; for the Lord your God, He is the One who goes with you. He will not leave you nor forsake you.

Suggested Common Language Meaning

Be strong you are not alone. God is with you and will never abandon you.

Notes: _____
_____
_____
_____
_____
_____
_____

Commitment to Change

Commitment to change is an agreement or pledge to dedicate oneself to a new course or effort. All skill development requires commitment to change.

Jeremiah 29:11 ESV

For I know the plans I have for you, declares the Lord, plans for welfare and not for evil, to give you a future and a hope.

Suggested Common Language Meaning

God has a plan for you for a great future for you of hope and wellbeing.

*Notes:*_____

_____
_____
_____
_____
_____
_____

Commitment to Change

Commitment to change is an agreement or pledge to dedicate oneself to a new course or effort. All skill development requires commitment to change.

1 Chronicles 16:34

Oh, give thanks to the Lord, for He is good! For His mercy endures forever.

Suggested Common Language Meaning

The Lord is merciful, loving and forgiving and his goodness is always available to us.

*Notes:*_____
_____
_____
_____
_____
_____
_____
_____

Commitment to Change

Commitment to change is an agreement or pledge to dedicate oneself to a new course or effort. All skill development requires commitment to change.

Joshua 1:9 NKJV

Have I not commanded you? Be strong and of good courage; do not be afraid, nor be dismayed, for the Lord your God is with you wherever you go."

Suggested Common Language Meaning

We are instructed to be courageous and strong, do not be down or give up, because the Lord is with us wherever we go.

*Notes:*_____
_____
_____
_____
_____
_____
_____

Commitment to Change

Commitment to change is an agreement or pledge to dedicate oneself to a new course or effort. All skill development requires commitment to change.

John 1:16 ESV

For from his fullness we have all
received, grace upon grace.

Suggested Common Language Meaning

God's mercies are given each day and todays mercies are given upon yesterdays. Grace was given by God in the beginning and further reveals by the Jesus. Thus we are each blessed with grace upon grace in each new day.

*Notes:*_____
_____
_____
_____
_____
_____

Commitment to Change

Commitment to change is an agreement or pledge to dedicate oneself to a new course or effort. All skill development requires commitment to change.

John 1:16 ESV

For from his fullness we have all received, grace upon grace.

Suggested Common Language Meaning

God's mercies are given each day and todays mercies are given upon yesterdays. Grace was given by God in the beginning and further reveals by the Jesus. Thus we are each blessed with grace upon grace.

*Notes:*_____
_____
_____
_____
_____
_____
_____
_____

Commitment to Change

Commitment to change is an agreement or pledge to dedicate oneself to a new course or effort. All skill development requires commitment to change.

Luke 1:37 NKJV

For with God nothing will be impossible.

Suggested Common Language Meaning

All things are possible with God as our helpmate.

*Notes:*_____

_____
_____
_____
_____
_____
_____
_____
_____

Commitment to Change

An agreement or pledge to dedicate oneself to a new course or effort. All skill development requires commitment to change.

Proverbs 14:15 NIV

The simple believe anything, but the prudent give thought to their steps.

Suggested Common Language Meaning

Be mindful and purposeful in your choices.

*Notes:*_____
_____
_____
_____
_____
_____
_____
_____

Commitment to Change

Commitment to change is an agreement or pledge to dedicate oneself to a new course or effort. All skill development requires commitment to change.

Proverbs 3:6 ESV

In all your ways acknowledge him, and he will make straight your paths.

Suggested Common Language Meaning

Be mindful of God's guidance and your way will be assisted.

*Notes:*_____
_____
_____
_____
_____
_____
_____
_____

Commitment to Change

Commitment to change is an agreement or pledge to dedicate oneself to a new course or effort. All skill development requires commitment to change.

Psalm 34:18 ESV

The Lord is near to the brokenhearted and saves the crushed in spirit.

Suggested Common Language Meaning

The more difficult the task the closer the Lord walks to us to offer us assistance, love and strength.

*Notes:*_____
_____
_____
_____
_____
_____
_____

Commitment to Change

Commitment to change is an agreement or pledge to dedicate oneself to a new course or effort. All skill development requires commitment to change.

Romans 5:1-5 NKJV

Therefore, having been justified by faith, we have peace with God through our Lord Jesus Christ, through whom also we have access by faith into this grace in which we stand, and rejoice in hope of the glory of God. And not only that, but we also glory in tribulations, knowing that tribulation produces perseverance; and perseverance, character; and character, hope. Now hope does not disappoint, because the love of God has been poured out in our hearts by the Holy Spirit who was given to us.

Suggested Common Language Meaning

In faith we have peace- tranquility, in faith we have access to grace- unmerited favor, and in hope- confidence knowing that which God has promised will come to pass. Even in our human troubles because difficulty develops perseverance, character and hope.

The hope promised is renewed by the Holy Spirit and is not empty but given freely as a blessing upon us.

*Notes:*_____
_____
_____
_____
_____
_____
_____
_____
_____
_____
_____
_____
_____
_____
_____
_____
_____
_____

Commitment to Change

Commitment to change is an agreement or pledge to dedicate oneself to a new course or effort. All skill development requires commitment to change.

Psalm 3:3 ESV

But you, O Lord, are a shield about me, my glory, and the lifter of my head.

Suggested Common Language Meaning

The Lord is my protection, the deepest source of my inner light, and what brings me through times of trouble.

Notes: _____
_____
_____
_____
_____
_____
_____
_____

Compassion

Compassion is a primary virtue taught by Jesus. Christian compassion means to feel empathy, mercy, sadness, sympathy, consideration, tenderness, and desire for improved conditions for another and to be with them in their life experience.

Isaiah 40:11 KJV

He will feed His flock like a shepherd. He will gather the lambs in His arms and carry them close to His heart. He will be gentle in leading those that are with young.

Suggested Common Language Meaning

The Lord provides tender loving care and attention. Carrying those who need carried. Leading those who need led, gently according to their ability.

*Notes:*_____
_____
_____
_____
_____

Compassion

Compassion is a primary virtue taught by Jesus. Christian compassion means to feel empathy, mercy, sadness, sympathy, consideration, tenderness, and desire for improved conditions for another and to be with them in their life experience.

Proverbs 21:21 ESV

Whoever pursues righteousness and kindness will find life, righteousness, and honor.

Suggested Common Language Meaning

Whoever acts in righteousness- Christ-like, right in thought, attitude, word and behavior, and kindness- tenderhearted, forgiving and patient, will find the miracle of life, in esteem and alignment with God's will.

*Notes:*_____
_____
_____
_____
_____
_____

Compassion

Compassion is a primary virtue taught by Jesus. Christian compassion means to feel empathy, mercy, sadness, sympathy, consideration, tenderness, and desire for improved conditions for another and to be with them in their life experience.

Proverbs 31:26 ESV

She opens her mouth with wisdom, and the teaching of kindness is on her tongue.

Suggested Common Language Meaning

Speak when it is wise, prudent and necessary, build up and be tenderhearted and gentle with others.

*Notes:*_____
_____
_____
_____
_____
_____
_____

Compassion

Compassion is a primary virtue taught by Jesus. Christian compassion means to feel empathy, mercy, sadness, sympathy, consideration, tenderness, and desire for improved conditions for another and to be with them in their life experience.

Ephesians 4:32 ESV

Be kind to one another, tenderhearted, forgiving one another, as God in Christ forgave you.

Suggested Common Language Meaning

Be kind, gentle, easy to get along with, forgiving and treat others with Christ-like forgiveness.

Notes:

Compassion

Compassion is a primary virtue taught by Jesus. Christian compassion means to feel empathy, mercy, sadness, sympathy, consideration, tenderness, and desire for improved conditions for another and to be with them in their life experience.

1 Peter 3:8-17 ESV

Finally, all of you, have unity of mind, sympathy, brotherly love, a tender heart, and a humble mind. Do not repay evil for evil or reviling for reviling, but on the contrary, bless, for to this you were called, that you may obtain a blessing.

Suggested Common Language Meaning

Be of one mind, in the Christ, considerate, loving one another, soft-hearted, and submissive to God's path or plan for you. Do not engage in immorality, corruption and discord. But strive to be a blessing, and in blessing others you will be blessed.

*Notes:*_____

_____

_____

Compassion

Compassion is a primary virtue taught by Jesus. Christian compassion means to feel empathy, mercy, sadness, sympathy, consideration, tenderness, and desire for improved conditions for another and to be with them in their life experience.

Matthew 7:1-2 ESV

Judge not, that you be not judged. For with the judgment you pronounce you will be judged, and with the measure you use it will be measured to you.

Suggested Common Language Meaning

Judging is not your job. Whatever you use as a measure of judgment against others will be used as a measure against you.

*Notes:*_____

_____
_____
_____
_____
_____
_____

Compassion

Compassion is a primary virtue taught by Jesus. Christian compassion means to feel empathy, mercy, sadness, sympathy, consideration, tenderness, and desire for improved conditions for another and to be with them in their life experience.

Romans 12:15 ESV

Rejoice with those who rejoice, weep with those who weep.

Suggested Common Language Meaning

Being with others in compassion means feeling them, wherever they are, and holding space for them to be as they are, without judgment.

*Notes:*_____
_____
_____
_____
_____
_____
_____

Compassion

Compassion is a primary virtue taught by Jesus. Christian compassion means to feel empathy, mercy, sadness, sympathy, consideration, tenderness, and desire for improved conditions for another and to be with them in their life experience.

Lamentations 3:22-23 ESV

The steadfast love of the LORD never ceases; his mercies never come to an end; they are new every morning; great is your faithfulness.

Suggested Common Language Meaning

The love, loving kindness, forgiveness, empathy and compassion of the Lord is enormous, constant and never ending.

*Notes:*_____
_____
_____
_____
_____

Crisis Survival

Crisis Survival helps tolerate painful events, urges, and emotions when you cannot make things better right away.

Deuteronomy 31:6 ICB

Be strong and brave. Don't be afraid of them. Don't be frightened. The Lord your God will go with you. He will not leave you or forget you.

Suggested Common Language Meaning

Be strong and brave in this moment, don't be scared because the Lord is with you and will never forget you or leave you.

*Notes:*_____
_____
_____
_____
_____
_____
_____

Crisis Survival

Crisis Survival helps tolerate painful events, urges, and emotions when you cannot make things better right away.

1 Chronicles 16:11 NLV

Look to the Lord and ask for His strength. Look to Him all the time.

Suggested Common Language Meaning

Do not rely only upon yourself at times of trouble but look to the Lord always and ask for strength.

*Notes:*_____
_____
_____
_____
_____
_____
_____
_____

Crisis Survival

Crisis Survival helps tolerate painful events, urges, and emotions when you cannot make things better right away.

Psalm 37:24 NLV

When he falls, he will not be thrown down, because the Lord holds his hand.

Suggested Common Language Meaning

When we fall in life we will not be broken because the Lord holds our hand. You are never left to fall because God is with you always.

*Notes:*_____
_____
_____
_____
_____
_____
_____

Crisis Survival

Crisis Survival helps tolerate painful events, urges, and emotions when you cannot make things better right away.

Ephesians 6:10 NET

Finally, be strengthened in the Lord and in the strength of his power.

Suggested Common Language Meaning

Let the capacity and power of the Lord assist and strengthen you.

*Notes:*_____
_____
_____
_____
_____
_____
_____
_____

Crisis Survival

Crisis Survival helps tolerate painful events, urges, and emotions when you cannot make things better right away.

Ephesians 6:10 NET

Finally, be strengthened in the Lord and in the strength of his power.

Suggested Common Language Meaning

Let the capacity and power of the Lord assist you and strengthen you.

*Notes:*_____
_____
_____
_____
_____
_____
_____

Crisis Survival

Crisis Survival helps tolerate painful events, urges, and emotions when you cannot make things better right away.

Deuteronomy 31:6 NET

Be strong and courageous! Do not fear or tremble before them, for the Lord your God is the one who is going with you. He will not fail you or abandon you!"

Suggested Common Language Meaning

Fortify yourself with the knowledge that you are not alone and need not be afraid. God is with you and he will not fail you or leave you.

*Notes:*_____
_____
_____
_____
_____
_____
_____
_____

Crisis Survival

Crisis Survival helps tolerate painful events, urges, and emotions when you cannot make things better right away.

Psalm 34:18 ESV

The Lord is near to the brokenhearted and saves the crushed in spirit.

Suggested Common Language Meaning

The Lord watches closely those who are having heartache so he can assist and support us.

*Notes:*_____
_____
_____
_____
_____
_____
_____
_____

Crisis Survival

Crisis Survival helps tolerate painful events, urges, and emotions when you cannot make things better right away.

1 Peter 5:7 ESV

Cast all your anxieties on him, because he cares for you.

Suggested Common Language Meaning

God promises to carry us and our burdens if we will ask. God waits to answer when we pray, to forgive us, to comfort us when we are in need. Ask for comfort at times of need.

*Notes:*_____
_____
_____
_____
_____
_____
_____
_____

Crisis Survival

Crisis Survival helps tolerate painful events, urges, and emotions when you cannot make things better right away.

Luke 1:37 ESV

For nothing will be impossible with God.

Suggested Common Language Meaning

All things are possible with God. Including this moment, challenge, difficulty, or pain.

*Notes:*_____
_____
_____
_____
_____
_____
_____
_____

Crisis Survival

Crisis Survival helps tolerate painful events, urges, and emotions when you cannot make things better right away.

Isaiah 26:3-4 ESV

You keep him in perfect peace, whose mind is stayed on you, because he trusts in you. Trust in the Lord forever, for the Lord God is an everlasting strength.

Suggested Common Language Meaning

God will keep you in perfect everlasting strength, keep your mind and trust upon him.

*Notes:*_____
_____
_____
_____
_____
_____
_____
_____

Crisis Survival

Crisis Survival helps tolerate painful events, urges, and emotions when you cannot make things better right away.

Psalm 31:24 NKJV

Be of good courage, and He shall strengthen your heart, all you who hope in the Lord.

Suggested Common Language Meaning

Be courageous! God will strengthen you if you place your hope upon him.

*Notes:*_____

Crisis Survival

Crisis Survival helps tolerate painful events, urges, and emotions when you cannot make things better right away.

Hebrews 4:16 ESV

Let us then with confidence draw near to the throne of grace, that we may receive mercy and find grace to help in time of need.

Suggested Common Language Meaning

Know that if you draw near to God you will receive grace and mercy in you time of difficulty.

Notes:_____
_____
_____
_____
_____
_____
_____
_____

Crisis Survival

Crisis Survival helps tolerate painful events, urges, and emotions when you cannot make things better right away.

Isaiah 41:10 ESV

Fear not, for I am with you; be not dismayed, for I am your God; I will strengthen you, I will help you, I will uphold you with my righteous right hand.

Suggested Common Language Meaning

Do not be afraid, do not be confused. God will strengthen, help and guide you.

Notes:_____
_____
_____
_____
_____
_____
_____
_____

Crisis Survival

Crisis Survival helps tolerate painful events, urges, and emotions when you cannot make things better right away.

Psalm 23:4 ESV

Even though I walk through the valley of the shadow of death, I will fear no evil, for you are with me; your rod and your staff, they comfort me.

Suggested Common Language Meaning

We are never alone. We always have a spiritual, invisible, means of support, even if we are physically alone or feel isolated, withdrawn or disconnected from others.

Notes:
_____
_____
_____
_____
_____
_____
_____

Crisis Survival

Crisis Survival helps tolerate painful events, urges, and emotions when you cannot make things better right away.

Psalm 147:3 ESV

He heals the brokenhearted and binds up their wounds.

Suggested Common Language Meaning

Christ is our spiritual medic. Recovery through the Holy Spirit who binds our brokenness, pain and wounds.

*Notes:*_____
_____
_____
_____
_____
_____
_____
_____

Crisis Survival

Crisis Survival helps tolerate painful events, urges, and emotions when you cannot make things better right away.

Psalm 62:8 ESV

Trust in him at all times, O people; pour out your heart before him; God is a refuge for us.

Suggested Common Language Meaning

Christ is our refuge. Share your burdens and trust in his loving care.

*Notes:*_____
_____
_____
_____
_____
_____
_____
_____

Crisis Survival

Crisis Survival helps tolerate painful events, urges, and emotions when you cannot make things better right away.

Psalm 121:1-2 ESV

A Song of Ascents. I lift up my eyes to the hills. From where does my help come? My help comes from the Lord, who made heaven and earth.

Suggested Common Language Meaning

This is a song of joyous labor with the invisible support system that is Christ.

Notes:_____
_____
_____
_____
_____
_____
_____

Crisis Survival

Crisis Survival helps tolerate painful events, urges, and emotions when you cannot make things better right away.

John 16:32 ESV

Behold, the hour is coming, indeed it has come, when you will be scattered, each to his own home, and will leave me alone. Yet I am not alone, for the Father is with me.

Suggested Common Language Meaning

While we are at times physically alone as everyone goes about their daily tasks, labors, homes. We are never alone, Christ is with us always.

Notes:_____
_____
_____
_____
_____
_____
_____

Crisis Survival

Crisis Survival helps tolerate painful events, urges, and emotions when you cannot make things better right away.

Matthew 11:28 ESV

Come to me, all who labor and are heavy laden, and I will give you rest.

Suggested Common Language Meaning

Christ is with us always and if we are heavy with responsibilities, fears, and cares of the world we can give them to him in full faith and trust and rest in the knowing that we can take a break from it.

*Notes:*_____
_____
_____
_____
_____
_____
_____

Crisis Survival

Crisis Survival helps tolerate painful events, urges, and emotions when you cannot make things better right away.

1 Chronicles 16:11 ESV

Seek the Lord and his strength; seek his presence continually!

Suggested Common Language Meaning

To search for, ask or consult in holy devotion the Lord's strength. To word as a goal to be in his holy presence in our heart and minds at all times.

*Notes:*_____
_____
_____
_____
_____
_____
_____
_____

Crisis Survival

Crisis Survival helps tolerate painful events, urges, and emotions when you cannot make things better right away.

Philippians 4:19 ESV

And my God will supply every need of yours according to his riches in glory in Christ Jesus.

Suggested Common Language Meaning

God is our source of everything. We are rich when we exalt and glorify our walk with Jesus.

*Notes:*_____
_____
_____
_____
_____
_____
_____

Crisis Survival

Crisis Survival helps tolerate painful events, urges, and emotions when you cannot make things better right away.

Romans 8:39 ESV

Nor height nor depth, nor anything else in all creation, will be able to separate us from the love of God in Christ Jesus our Lord.

Suggested Common Language Meaning

There is nothing that can separate us from the love of God. We are always loves, and there is no behavior that is so great or terrible that the love of God through Christ that can separate us from this birthright. God loves when we realize we are off our path and find our way back to him.

*Notes:*_____
_____
_____
_____

Crisis Survival

Crisis Survival helps tolerate painful events, urges, and emotions when you cannot make things better right away.

Jeremiah 29:11 ESV

For I know the plans I have for you, declares the Lord, plans for welfare and not for evil, to give you a future and a hope.

Suggested Common Language Meaning

We are divinely inspired to our path by the Lord. It is a path or welfare, promise and hope.

*Notes:*_____
_____
_____
_____
_____
_____
_____

Compromise

DEAR MAN Negotiate and be open to compromise to address challenging situations. Focus on opportunities provided by difficult conversations and be aware of potential conflicts, conflicting needs, wants and values. Compromise is more likely to leave both parties feeling good about the challenge.

Philippians 2:4 ESV

Let each of you look not only to his own interests, but also to the interests of others.

Suggested Common Language Meaning

Be mindful of your interests, as well as those of others.

*Notes:*_____

_____
_____
_____
_____
_____
_____
_____

Compromise

DEAR MAN Negotiate and be open to compromise to address challenging situations. Focus on opportunities provided by difficult conversations and be aware of potential conflicts, conflicting needs, wants and values. Compromise is more likely to leave both parties feeling good about the challenge.

Acts 20:35 ESV

In all things I have shown you that by working hard in this way we must help the weak and remember the words of the Lord Jesus, how he himself said, 'It is more blessed to give than to receive.

Suggested Common Language Meaning

Be helpful, kind and generous. Giving is good for the giver and receiver.

*Notes:*_____
_____
_____
_____
_____

Dialectics

Dialectics is the understanding, and effort toward synthesis, that many things in the world are seemingly opposites.

Romans 5:20-21 NLT

Moreover the law entered that the offense might abound. But where sin abounded, grace abounded much more, so that as sin reigned in death, even so grace might reign through righteousness to eternal life through Jesus Christ our Lord.

Suggested Common Language Meaning

This verse is an example of dialectics- where there is falling short there is also grace. Where there is death, eternal life. Each being true in any given moment but also seemingly opposed.

Notes:_____
_____
_____
_____
_____
_____

Dialectics

Dialectics is the understanding, and effort toward synthesis, that many things in the world are seemingly opposites.

Ephesians 2:10 NKJV

For we are His workmanship, created in Christ Jesus for good works, which God prepared beforehand that we should walk in them.

Suggested Common Language Meaning

This verse is an example of dialectics- we are created in divine and live in the world which is mundane.

*Notes:*_____
_____
_____
_____
_____
_____
_____
_____

Dialectics

Dialectics is the understanding, and effort toward synthesis, that many things in the world are seemingly opposites.

Job 31:6 ESV

Let me be weighed in a just balance, and let God know my integrity!

Suggested Common Language Meaning

To be in balanced in Wise Mind allows us to live with integrity. Strive to demonstrate integrity.

*Notes:*_____
_____
_____
_____
_____
_____
_____
_____

Dialectics

Dialectics is the understanding, and effort toward synthesis, that many things in the world are seemingly opposites.

Proverbs 16:3 NKJV

Commit your works to the Lord, and your thoughts will be established.

Suggested Common Language Meaning

This passage is about intention. Intend yourself to skillful efforts and your thoughts will come along. It is about the dialectic of choosing actions, in spite of urges.

*Notes:*_____
_____
_____
_____
_____
_____
_____
_____

Dialectics

Dialectics is the understanding, and effort toward synthesis, that many things in the world are seemingly opposites.

1 Corinthians 10:13 ESV

No temptation has overtaken you that is not common to man. God is faithful, and he will not let you be tempted beyond your ability, but with the temptation he will also provide the way of escape, that you may be able to endure it.

Suggested Common Language Meaning

Temptation is a normal everyday life experience. And, God will give you strength to endure the challenge or escape.

*Notes:*_____
_____
_____
_____
_____
_____
_____

Decrease Vulnerability

Decreasing vulnerability help us reduce our baseline so there is more capacity before overwhelm.

James 1:26 ESV

If anyone thinks he is religious and does not bridle his tongue but deceives his heart, this person's religion is worthless.

Suggested Common Language Meaning

Be mindful of your thoughts and speech when you are not overwhelmed so that practice is easier to maintain at times of distress.

*Notes:*_____
_____
_____
_____
_____
_____
_____
_____

Distress Tolerance

Distress tolerance skills increase our ability to deal with life's stressors, grievances and losses without being overwhelmed by them.

Proverbs 24:16 ESV

For the righteous falls seven times and rises again, but the wicked stumble in times of calamity.

Suggested Common Language Meaning

Keep going in righteousness. Own your behavior and hold yourself to account when you fall short. Strive to be the best person you can be.

*Notes:*_____

_____
_____
_____
_____
_____
_____
_____

Distress Tolerance

Distress tolerance skills increase our ability to deal with life's stressors, grievances and losses without being overwhelmed by them.

James 1:3 ESV

For you know that the testing of your faith produces steadfastness.

Suggested Common Language Meaning

Calm seas do not make a skillful sailor. Prepare yourself to be challenged, and be steadfast in your faith and skills. If you fall short, right yourself and keep trying.

*Notes:*_____

_____
_____
_____
_____
_____
_____
_____

Distress Tolerance

Distress tolerance skills increase our ability to deal with life's stressors, grievances and losses without being overwhelmed by them.

Joshua 10:25 NKJV

Then Joshua said to them, "Do not be afraid, nor be dismayed; be strong and of good courage, for thus the LORD will do to all your enemies against whom you fight."

Suggested Common Language Meaning

Be strong and of good courage, should be distress tolerance's motto!

*Notes:*_____
_____
_____
_____
_____
_____
_____

Distress Tolerance

Distress tolerance skills increase our ability to deal with life's stressors, grievances and losses without being overwhelmed by them.

Proverbs 12:16 ESV

The vexation of a fool is known at once, but the prudent ignores an insult.

Suggested Common Language Meaning

Do not be annoyed, frustrated or worried, but act with care, ignoring those who might speak against you or try to upset you.

*Notes:*_____

_____

_____

_____

_____

_____

_____

_____

E

Effectively

Effectively means to do what works.

Titus 1:8 ESV

But hospitable, a lover of good, self-controlled, upright, holy, and disciplined.

Suggested Common Language Meaning

Be easy to get along with, love that which is good, be self-controlled, honest and honorable. Demonstrate your ability to control yourself regardless of the circumstance.

Notes: _____

_____
_____
_____
_____
_____
_____
_____
_____

Effectively

Effectively means to do what works.

Ephesians 4:24

You must become a new person and be God-like. Then you will be made right with God and have a true holy life.

Suggested Common Language Meaning

Be new in your person. Be God-like, whatever that means to you. Be honest, courageous, dependable, calm and gracious.

Notes: _____
_____
_____
_____
_____
_____
_____
_____

Effectively

Effectively means to do what works.

2 Timothy 1:7 ESV

For God gave us a spirit not of fear but of power and love and self-control.

Suggested Common Language Meaning

Focus upon your inner strength, which is a divine gift, of personal power, love and self-control.

*Notes:*_____

_____
_____
_____
_____
_____
_____
_____

Effectively

Effectively means to do what works.

Proverbs 14:29 ESV

Whoever is slow to anger has great understanding, but he who has a hasty temper exalts folly.

Suggested Common Language Meaning

Be slow to get angry and seek to understand. A person with a temper will make needless mistakes in judgment.

*Notes:*_____

_____
_____
_____
_____
_____
_____
_____

Effectively

Effectively means to do what works.

Romans 13:7 ESV

Pay to all what is owed to them: taxes to whom taxes are owed, revenue to whom revenue is owed, respect to whom respect is owed, honor to whom honor is owed.

Suggested Common Language Meaning

Take care of responsibilities, be respectful, and go along to get along.

*Notes:*_____

_____
_____
_____
_____
_____
_____
_____

Embrace Change

Embracing change is critical to wellbeing, as some things remain constant, change is a basis of all life. Every day there is change and the acceptance of it is critical to skillful application of the self to daily life.

Isaiah 26:3 NKJV

You will keep him in perfect peace,
whose mind is stayed on you, because he trusts in you.

Suggested Common Language Meaning

Have faith that the Lord trusts you to be able to manage the changes and challenges you come to in your life.

*Notes:*_____

_____
_____
_____
_____
_____
_____
_____

Emotion Mind

Emotion mind is when our thoughts and based purely in emotion. Feeling emotions is necessary to effectively, skillfully and fully managing them.

Ecclesiastes 3:4-6 NKJV

A time to weep, And a time to laugh; A time to mourn, And a time to dance; time to cast away stones, And a time to gather stones; A time to embrace, And a time to refrain from embracing; A time to gain, And a time to lose; A time to keep, And a time to throw away;

Suggested Common Language Meaning

All feelings have a time. They are normal and natural.

Notes:_____
_____
_____
_____
_____
_____
_____
_____

Emotion Mind

Emotion mind is when our thoughts and based purely in emotion. Feeling emotions is necessary to effectively, skillfully and fully managing them.

Proverbs 17:22 NKJV

A merry heart does good, like medicine, but a broken spirit dries the bones.

Suggested Common Language Meaning

Strive to have a merry heart. It will make life easier. Practicing a broken, downtrodden spirit is exhausting and self-perpetuating.

*Notes:*_____

_____
_____
_____
_____
_____
_____
_____

Emotional Regulation

Emotion regulation is to effectively, skillfully and fully manage emotions.

Galatians 5:22-23

But the fruit of the Spirit is love, joy, peace, patience, kindness, goodness, faithfulness, gentleness, and self-control. Against such things there is no law.

Suggested Common Language Meaning

Strive to develop love, joy, peace, patience, kindness, goodness, faithfulness, gentleness, and self-control in your life every day.

*Notes:*_____
_____
_____
_____
_____
_____
_____
_____

Emotional Regulation

Emotion regulation is to effectively, skillfully and fully manage emotions.

Titus 2:12 ESV

Training us to renounce ungodliness and worldly passions, and to live self-controlled, upright, and godly lives in the present age,

Suggested Common Language Meaning

Strive to develop self-controlled, upright, and godly life daily.

*Notes:*_____
_____
_____
_____
_____
_____
_____
_____

Emotional Regulation

Emotion regulation is to effectively, skillfully and fully manage emotions.

Philippians 4:8 ESV

Finally, brothers, whatever is true, whatever is honorable, whatever is just, whatever is pure, whatever is lovely, whatever is commendable, if there is any excellence, if there is anything worthy of praise, think about these things.

Suggested Common Language Meaning

Strive to develop honor, justice, purity, loveliness, commendable, and excellence worthy of praise in your life in all things.

*Notes:*_____
_____
_____
_____
_____
_____
_____
_____

Emotional Regulation

Emotion regulation is to effectively, skillfully and fully manage emotions.

Colossians 3:8 ESV

But now you must put them all away: anger, wrath, malice, slander, and obscene talk from your mouth.

Suggested Common Language Meaning

Strive to not speak or act in anger, wrath, malice, slander, and obscene talk.

*Notes:*_____
_____
_____
_____
_____
_____
_____
_____

F

FAST

FAST is the skill of be Fair, no Apologies for existing, Stick to your values, be Truthful.

Colossians 4:6 ESV

Let your speech always be gracious, seasoned with salt, so that you may know how you ought to answer each person.

Suggested Common Language Meaning

Be Fair: Be gracious and truthful.

*Notes:*_____

_____
_____
_____
_____
_____
_____

FAST

FAST is the skill of be Fair, no Apologies for existing, Stick to your values, be Truthful.

Zechariah 7:9 ESV

Thus says the LORD of hosts, render true judgments, show kindness and mercy to one another.

Suggested Common Language Meaning

Be Fair: Be true, kind and gentle with self and others.

*Notes:*_____
_____
_____
_____
_____
_____
_____
_____

FAST

FAST is the skill of be Fair, no Apologies for existing, Stick to your values, be Truthful.

Exodus 23:6 NLV

Do not keep from doing what is right and fair in trying to help a poor brother when he has a problem.

Suggested Common Language Meaning

Be Fair: Do what is right and fair. Help others when they are in need.

*Notes:*_____
_____
_____
_____
_____
_____
_____

FAST

FAST is the skill of be Fair, no Apologies for existing, Stick to your values, be Truthful.

Deuteronomy 25:15-17 NET

You must have an accurate and correct stone weight and an accurate and correct measuring container, so that your life may be extended in the land the LORD your God is about to give you. For anyone who acts dishonestly in these ways is abhorrent to the LORD your God.

Suggested Common Language Meaning

Be Fair: Be honest.

*Notes:*_____

_____
_____
_____
_____
_____
_____
_____

FAST

FAST is the skill of be Fair, no Apologies for existing, Stick to your values, be Truthful.

Luke 6:31 ESV

And as you wish that others would do to you, do so to them.

Suggested Common Language Meaning

Be Fair: Treat others the way you wish to be treated.

*Notes:*_____
_____
_____
_____
_____
_____
_____
_____

FAST

FAST is the skill of be Fair, no Apologies for existing, Stick to your values, be Truthful.

Micah 6:8 NLV

O man, He has told you what is good. What does the Lord ask of you but to do what is fair and to love kindness, and to walk without pride with your God?

Suggested Common Language Meaning

Be Fair: Do what you know is good, be fair, act with loving kindness and do not be prideful.

*Notes:*_____

_____

_____

_____

_____

_____

_____

_____

FAST

FAST is the skill of be Fair, no Apologies for existing, Stick to your values, be Truthful.

James 5:16 ASV

Confess therefore your sins one to another, and pray one for another, that ye may be healed. The supplication of a righteous man availeth much in its working.

Suggested Common Language Meaning

No unnecessary Apologies: Apologize and make amends when appropriate

*Notes:*_____

_____
_____
_____
_____
_____
_____
_____

FAST

FAST is the skill of be Fair, no Apologies for existing, Stick to your values, be Truthful.

Proverbs 11:3 ESV

The integrity of the upright guides them, but the crookedness of the treacherous destroys them.

Suggested Common Language Meaning

Stick to values: Be upright in integrity. Integrity is the quality of being honest and having strong moral principles; moral uprightness.

*Notes:*_____
_____
_____
_____
_____
_____
_____
_____

FAST

FAST is the skill of be Fair, no Apologies for existing, Stick to your values, be Truthful.

1 Corinthians 16:14 ESV

Let all that you do be done in love.

Suggested Common Language Meaning

Stick to values: Do what you do, with love. There is no room with love for spite, revenge, anger, pride, ect..

*Notes:*_____

_____

_____

_____

_____

_____

_____

_____

FAST

FAST is the skill of be Fair, no Apologies for existing, Stick to your values, be Truthful.

Proverbs 14:5 NKJV

A faithful witness does not lie, but a false witness will utter lies.

Suggested Common Language Meaning

Truthfulness: Be truthful, and upstanding. Do not lie, exaggerate or create drama.

*Notes:*_____
_____
_____
_____
_____
_____
_____
_____

FAST

FAST is the skill of be Fair, no Apologies for existing, Stick to your values, be Truthful.

Psalm 141:3 ESV

Set a guard, O LORD, over my mouth; keep watch over the door of my lips!

Suggested Common Language Meaning

Truthfulness: Be mindful or your speech and ask the Lord for help if you need.

Notes:_____
_____
_____
_____
_____
_____
_____

FAST

FAST is the skill of be Fair, no Apologies for existing, Stick to your values, be Truthful.

2 Corinthians 6:6-7 ESV

By purity, knowledge, patience, kindness, the Holy Spirit, genuine love; by truthful speech, and the power of God; with the weapons of righteousness for the right hand and for the left;

Suggested Common Language Meaning

Truthfulness: God's power is working in you and you have fruits of the Spirit,, including purity, knowledge, patience, kindness, genuine love, and truthfulness. You can embody all these things when righteousness is you weapon.

*Notes:*_____
_____
_____
_____
_____
_____
_____

FAST

FAST is the skill of be Fair, no Apologies for existing, Stick to your values, be Truthful.

James 1:26 ESV

If anyone thinks he is religious and does not bridle his tongue but deceives his heart, this person's religion is worthless.

Suggested Common Language Meaning

Truthfulness: Mind your speech, do not be a deceiver in your heart. To omit, is also a lie.

Notes:_____
_____
_____
_____
_____
_____
_____
_____

Fear

Fear is an unpleasant internal experience or threat of danger, risk, loss, pain.

Philippians 4:6-9 NIV

Do not be anxious about anything, but in every situation, by prayer and petition, with thanksgiving, present your requests to God. And the peace of God, which transcends all understanding, will guard your hearts and your minds in Christ Jesus.

Suggested Common Language Meaning

Pray with gratitude, and not with fear or anxiety, in all things and be at peace in your heart and mind because it is in God's hands and there is nothing to be worried about.

*Notes:*_____
_____
_____
_____
_____
_____
_____

Fear

Fear is an unpleasant internal experience or threat of danger, risk, loss, pain.

1 Peter 5:7 ESV

Casting all your anxieties on him, because he cares for you.

Suggested Common Language Meaning

Let go and let God.

*Notes:*_____

_____
_____
_____
_____
_____
_____
_____

Fear

Fear is an unpleasant internal experience or threat of danger, risk, loss, pain.

2 Timothy 1:7 ESV

For God gave us a spirit not of fear but of power and love and self-control.

Suggested Common Language Meaning

God gave us the capacity of power, love and self-control. Whether we choose to practice them is up to us.

*Notes:*_____

_____
_____
_____
_____
_____
_____
_____

Fear

Fear is an unpleasant internal experience or threat of danger, risk, loss, pain.

Deuteronomy 31:6 ESV

Be strong and courageous. Do not fear or be in dread of them, for it is the LORD your God who goes with you. He will not leave you or forsake you.

Suggested Common Language Meaning

Be strong and courageous, and do not fear, because God is with you, and will never abandon you.

*Notes:*_____

_____
_____
_____
_____
_____
_____
_____

Fear

Fear is an unpleasant internal experience or threat of danger, risk, loss, pain.

Psalm 56:5 NAB

I praise the word of God; I trust in God, I do not fear. What can mere flesh do to me?

Suggested Common Language Meaning

No one can hurt you if you walk with God.

Notes:

Fear

Fear is an unpleasant internal experience or threat of danger, risk, loss, pain.

John 14:27 ESV

Peace I leave with you; my peace I give to you. Not as the world gives do I give to you. Let not your hearts be troubled, neither let them be afraid.

Suggested Common Language Meaning

Be at peace, do not be troubled or afraid as the Lord is with you always and heavenly gifts are poured upon you.

*Notes:*_____

_____
_____
_____
_____
_____
_____
_____

Fear

Fear is an unpleasant internal experience or threat of danger, risk, loss, pain.

Philippians 4:6-7 ESV

Do not be anxious about anything, but in everything by prayer and supplication with thanksgiving let your requests be made known to God. And the peace of God, which surpasses all understanding, will guard your hearts and your minds in Christ Jesus.

Suggested Common Language Meaning

Do not be afraid, but pray and submit yourself to God, And the peace of God, will guard your heart and mind.

Notes:_____

_____
_____
_____
_____
_____
_____
_____

Fear

Fear is an unpleasant internal experience or threat of danger, risk, loss, pain.

Job 3:25 NASB

For what I fear comes upon me, and what I dread befalls me.

Suggested Common Language Meaning

If you fear and dread, then your life will be fear and dread.

*Notes:*_____

_____
_____
_____
_____
_____
_____
_____

G

GIVE

GIVE is the relationship effectiveness skill of be gentle, be interested, be validating and have an easy manner.

1 John 4:7-8 ESV

Gentle Beloved, let us love one another, for love is from God, and whoever loves has been born of God and knows God. Anyone who does not love does not know God, because God is love.

Suggested Common Language Meaning

Gentle: To be Godly is to love. Love is gentle, love is kind, love is patient.

*Notes:*_____

_____

_____

_____

_____

_____

_____

GIVE

GIVE is the relationship effectiveness skill of be gentle, be interested, be validating and have an easy manner.

Proverbs 8:34 ESV

Blessed is the one who listens to me, watching daily at my gates, waiting beside my doors.

Suggested Common Language Meaning

Interested: Be observant to be blessed.

*Notes:*_____

_____

_____

_____

_____

_____

_____

_____

GIVE

GIVE is the relationship effectiveness skill of be gentle, be interested, be validating and have an easy manner.

Ephesians 4:25 NIV

Therefore each of you must put off falsehood and speak truthfully to your neighbor, for we are all members of one body.

Suggested Common Language Meaning

Validate: Speak truthfully and mindfully, because we are all a part of a greater whole, the body of Christ.

*Notes:*_____
_____
_____
_____
_____
_____
_____

GIVE

GIVE is the relationship effectiveness skill of be gentle, be interested, be validating and have an easy manner.

Ephesians 4:32 ESV

Be kind to one another, tenderhearted, forgiving one another, as God in Christ forgave you.

Suggested Common Language Meaning

Easy manner: Be kind, tenderhearted and forgive, as you have been forgiven.

*Notes:*_____

_____
_____
_____
_____
_____
_____
_____
_____

GIVE

GIVE is the relationship effectiveness skill of be gentle, be interested, be validating and have an easy manner.

Ephesians 4:29 ESV

Let no corrupting talk come out of your mouths, but only such as is good for building up, as fits the occasion, that it may give grace to those who hear.

Suggested Common Language Meaning

Easy manner: Be mindful of your speech. Let it be of good character, building others up, appropriate to the situation, setting and audience, expressing goodwill and generosity.

*Notes:*_____
_____
_____
_____
_____
_____
_____
_____

GIVE

GIVE is the relationship effectiveness skill of be gentle, be interested, be validating and have an easy manner.

Proverbs 15:1 ESV

A soft answer turns away wrath, but a harsh word stirs up anger.

Suggested Common Language Meaning

Easy manner: Be mindful of your speech. Be easy and do not stir up anger unnecessarily.

*Notes:*_____
_____
_____
_____
_____
_____
_____
_____

GIVE

GIVE is the relationship effectiveness skill of be gentle, be interested, be validating and have an easy manner.

Proverbs 17:1 ESV

Better is a dry morsel with quiet than a house full of feasting with strife.

Suggested Common Language Meaning

Easy manner: Be mindful of your speech. Are you choosing quiet or stress, distress and drama?

*Notes:*_____
_____
_____
_____
_____
_____
_____

GIVE

GIVE is the relationship effectiveness skill of be gentle, be interested, be validating and have an easy manner.

Ephesians 4:26 ESV

Be angry and do not sin; do not let the sun go down on your anger.

Suggested Common Language Meaning

Easy manner: Being emotional is not an excuse to do what you know to be wrong. Deal with anger promptly, making any repairs, apologies or corrections that need to be made.

*Notes:*_____
_____
_____
_____
_____
_____
_____
_____

Guilt

Guilt is the emotion of 'I did a bad thing'.

Romans 3:23 ESV

For all have sinned and fall short of the glory of God,

Suggested Common Language Meaning

No one is perfect. All fall short at times. Acknowledge the failure, short coming, or sin and move on.

Notes:_____
_____
_____
_____
_____
_____
_____
_____

Guilt

Guilt is the emotion of 'I did a bad thing'.

1 John 2:1 ESV

My little children, I am writing these things to you so that you may not sin. But if anyone does sin, we have an advocate with the Father, Jesus Christ the righteous.

Suggested Common Language Meaning

Do not intentionally sin, but if you do Christ is on your side, let him help you.

*Notes:*_____
_____
_____
_____
_____
_____
_____
_____
_____

Guilt

Guilt is the emotion of 'I did a bad thing'.

Isaiah 6:7 ESV

And he touched my mouth and said: "Behold, this has touched your lips; your guilt is taken away, and your sin atoned for."

Suggested Common Language Meaning

Be touched by Christ in asking forgiveness and Christ will take your sin away.

Notes:_____
_____
_____
_____
_____
_____
_____
_____

Guilt

Guilt is the emotion of 'I did a bad thing'.

2 Corinthians 5:17 ESV

Therefore, if anyone is in Christ, he is a new creation. The old has passed away; behold, the new has come.

Suggested Common Language Meaning

Ask forgiveness and become a new creation in Christ.

*Notes:*_____
_____
_____
_____
_____
_____
_____
_____

Guilt

Guilt is the emotion of 'I did a bad thing'.

Hebrews 8:12 ESV

For I will be merciful toward their iniquities, and I will remember their sins no more.

Suggested Common Language Meaning

Christ tells us that he will be kind towards us when we fall short and once forgiven the sin is gone.

*Notes:*_____
_____
_____
_____
_____
_____
_____
_____

Guilt

Guilt is the emotion of 'I did a bad thing'.

Romans 2:1-29 ESV

Therefore you have no excuse, O man, every one of you who judges. For in passing judgment on another you condemn yourself, because you, the judge, practice the very same things. We know that the judgment of God rightly falls on those who practice such things. Do you suppose, O man—you who judge those who practice such things and yet do them yourself—that you will escape the judgment of God? Or do you presume on the riches of his kindness and forbearance and patience, not knowing that God's kindness is meant to lead you to repentance? But because of your hard and impenitent heart you are storing up wrath for yourself on the day of wrath when God's righteous judgment will be revealed. ...

Suggested Common Language Meaning

Do not judge in others that which you do yourself.

Notes:_____
_____
_____

H

Hope

Hope is an internal subjective experience of looking for something positive to transpire.

Matthew 19:26 KJV

But Jesus beheld them, and said unto them, with men this is impossible; but with God all things are possible.

Suggested Common Language Meaning

With God all things are possible.

*Notes:*_____

_____
_____
_____
_____
_____
_____
_____
_____

I

Interpersonal Effectiveness

Interpersonal effectiveness skills help us get along with others.

1 John 4:20-21 ESV

If anyone says, "I love God," and hates his brother, he is a liar; for he who does not love his brother whom he has seen cannot love God whom he has not seen. And this commandment we have from him: whoever loves God must also love his brother.

Suggested Common Language Meaning

We are commanded to love others as we love ourselves.

*Notes:*_____
_____
_____
_____
_____
_____
_____
_____
_____

Interpersonal Effectiveness

Interpersonal effectiveness skills help us get along with others.

Ephesians 4: 32 ESV

Be kind to one another, tenderhearted, forgiving one another, as God in Christ forgave you.

Suggested Common Language Meaning

Be kind, gentle and forgiving, as you are forgiven.

*Notes:*_____

_____
_____
_____
_____
_____
_____

Interpersonal Effectiveness

Interpersonal effectiveness skills help us get along with others.

1 Timothy 6:3-7 ESV

If anyone teaches a different doctrine and does not agree with the sound words of our Lord Jesus Christ and the teaching that accords with godliness, he is puffed up with conceit and understands nothing. He has an unhealthy craving for controversy and for quarrels about words, which produce envy, dissension, slander, evil suspicions, and constant friction among people who are depraved in mind and deprived of the truth, imagining that godliness is a means of gain. But godliness with contentment is great gain, for we brought nothing into the world, and we cannot take anything out of the world.

Suggested Common Language Meaning

To be godly do not crave disagreement, jealousy, lies, suspiciousness and difficulty getting along with others.

*Notes:*_____
_____
_____

Interpersonal Effectiveness

Interpersonal effectiveness skills help us get along with others.

Ephesians 4:32 ESV

Be kind to one another, tenderhearted, forgiving one another, as God in Christ forgave you.

Suggested Common Language Meaning

Be kind, gentle, easy to get along with, and quick to forgive.

*Notes:*_____

_____
_____
_____
_____
_____
_____
_____
_____

Interpersonal Effectiveness

Interpersonal effectiveness skills help us get along with others.

1 Peter 3:8 NKJV

Finally, all of you be of one mind, having compassion for one another; love as brothers, be tenderhearted, be courteous;

Suggested Common Language Meaning

Have compassion, brotherly love, be easy to get along with, with joy for others in your heart, be courteous.

*Notes:*_____
_____
_____
_____
_____
_____
_____
_____
_____

Interpersonal Effectiveness

Interpersonal effectiveness skills help us get along with others.

Matthew 9:36 NKJV

But when He saw the multitudes, He was moved with compassion for them, because they were weary and scattered, like sheep having no shepherd.

Suggested Common Language Meaning

Cultivate compassion for others as Christ had compassion for the multitude.

Notes:_____
_____
_____
_____
_____
_____
_____
_____
_____

Interpersonal Effectiveness

Interpersonal effectiveness skills help us get along with others.

Ephesians 4:31-32

Put out of your life all these things: bad feelings about other people, anger, temper, loud talk, bad talk which hurts other people, and bad feelings which hurt other people. You must be kind to each other. Think of the other person. Forgive other people just as God forgave you because of Christ's death on the cross.

Suggested Common Language Meaning

Be mindful to manage your thoughts and practice not having bad feelings about others, be slow to anger, do not be loud or speak bad language, which might hurt others. Think of others. Be kind and forgive, often and easily.

Notes: _____
_____
_____
_____
_____

J

Joy

Joy is the internal subjective feeling of happiness.

Luke 1:47 NKJV

And my spirit has rejoiced in God my Savior.

Suggested Common Language Meaning

You need no other reason to be happy because you can rejoice in your salvation.

*Notes:*_____
_____
_____
_____
_____
_____
_____
_____
_____

Joy

Joy is the internal subjective feeling of happiness.

Ecclesiastes 3:12 ESV

I perceived that there is nothing better for them than to be joyful and to do good as long as they live;

Suggested Common Language Meaning

Be joyful and do good, every day.

Notes:_____
_____
_____
_____
_____
_____
_____
_____
_____

Joy

Joy is the internal subjective feeling of happiness.

Psalm 16:11 ESV

You make known to me the path of life; in your presence there is fullness of joy; at your right hand are pleasures forevermore.

Suggested Common Language Meaning

God makes the path of our lives known to us and in his presences there is joy and pleasure forever.

Notes:_____
_____
_____
_____
_____
_____
_____
_____
_____
_____

L

Lighten your load

Lighten your load is a skill focused on allowing help at times of need.

Matthew 11:28 ESV

Come to me, all who labor and are heavy laden, and I will give you rest.

Suggested Common Language Meaning

Let go and let God give you peace of mind.

*Notes:*_____

_____
_____
_____
_____
_____
_____
_____
_____
_____

Letting go

Letting go is a skill focused on allowing.

Philippians 3:13-14 ESV

Brothers, I do not consider that I have made it my own. But one thing I do: forgetting what lies behind and straining forward to what lies ahead, I press on toward the goal for the prize of the upward call of God in Christ Jesus.

Suggested Common Language Meaning

Remember that God is always available to help with life's burdens.

*Notes:*_____
_____
_____
_____
_____
_____
_____
_____

Letting go

Letting go is a skill focused on allowing.

Matthew 11:28 ESV

Come to me, all who labor and are heavy laden, and I will give you rest.

Suggested Common Language Meaning

Feel at peace with God, lay your burdens upon him and rest.

*Notes:*_____

_____
_____
_____
_____
_____
_____
_____
_____
_____

Loving kindness

Loving kindness is an interpersonal skill of being kind and loving, because everyone is just human.

Roman 9:15-17 NLV

God said to Moses, "I will have loving-kindness and loving-pity for anyone I want to." These good things from God are not given to someone because he wants them or works to get them. They are given because of His loving-kindness.

Suggested Common Language Meaning

Loving kindness and loving-pity are gifts of the spirit and cannot be earned as they are given freely.

*Notes:*_____
_____
_____
_____
_____
_____
_____
_____

Loving kindness

Loving kindness is an interpersonal skill of being kind and loving, because everyone is just human.

Titus 3:2 ESV

To speak evil of no one, to avoid quarreling, to be gentle, and to show perfect courtesy toward all people.

Suggested Common Language Meaning

Strive to be good, gentle in your speak, and courteous to everyone.

*Notes:*_____
_____
_____
_____
_____
_____
_____
_____
_____

M

Making Repairs

Making repairs is an interpersonal skill of being correcting when we harm someone.

James 4:17 ESV

So whoever knows the right thing to do and fails to do it, for him it is sin.

Suggested Common Language Meaning

Willfulness to do what is right is not skillful.

*Notes:*_____

_____
_____
_____
_____
_____
_____
_____
_____

Meditate

Meditate is the skill of thinking deeply or focus one's mind for a period of time, in silence or with the aid of words or music, for religious or spiritual purposes or as a method of relaxation.

Psalm 119:15 ESV

I will meditate on your precepts and fix my eyes on your ways.

Suggested Common Language Meaning

Meditate on the ways of the Lord.

*Notes:*_____
_____
_____
_____
_____
_____
_____
_____
_____

Mindfulness

Mindfulness is the skillful mental state of focused awareness on the present moment, while nonjudgmentally, calmly acknowledging and accepting emotions, feelings, thoughts, and bodily sensations; the quality or state of being consciously purposefully aware of something.

Philippians 1:9-11 NIV

And this is my prayer: that your love may abound more and more in knowledge and depth of insight, so that you may be able to discern what is best and may be pure and blameless for the day of Christ, filled with the fruit of righteousness that comes through Jesus Christ—to the glory and praise of God.

Suggested Common Language Meaning

Knowledge, depth of insight and discernment are Christian mindfulness. Practice these skills to experience the fruit of righteousness.

*Notes:*_____
_____
_____
_____

Mindfulness

Mindfulness is the skillful mental state of focused awareness on the present moment, while nonjudgmentally, calmly acknowledging and accepting emotions, feelings, thoughts, and bodily sensations; the quality or state of being consciously purposefully aware of something.

Philippians 4:8 NIV

Finally, brothers and sisters, whatever is true, whatever is noble, whatever is right, whatever is pure, whatever is lovely, whatever is admirable—if anything is excellent or praiseworthy—think about such things.

Suggested Common Language Meaning

'Think on these things' directly relates to thought management. Be the boss of your brain.

*Notes:*_____
_____
_____
_____
_____
_____

Mindfulness

Mindfulness is the skillful mental state of focused awareness on the present moment, while nonjudgmentally, calmly acknowledging and accepting emotions, feelings, thoughts, and bodily sensations; the quality or state of being consciously purposefully aware of something.

Proverbs 25:28 ESV

A man without self-control is like a city broken into and left without walls.

Suggested Common Language Meaning

The ability to control one's behavior begins in controlling thoughts.

*Notes:*_____
_____
_____
_____
_____
_____
_____
_____

Mindfulness

Mindfulness is the skillful mental state of focused awareness on the present moment, while nonjudgmentally, calmly acknowledging and accepting emotions, feelings, thoughts, and bodily sensations; the quality or state of being consciously purposefully aware of something.

Proverbs 25:28 ESV

A man without self-control is like a city broken into and left without walls.

Suggested Common Language Meaning

Self-control begins in controlling your thoughts, which requires practiced mindfulness.

*Notes:*_____
_____
_____
_____
_____
_____
_____
_____

Mindfulness

Mindfulness is the skillful mental state of focused awareness on the present moment, while nonjudgmentally, calmly acknowledging and accepting emotions, feelings, thoughts, and bodily sensations; the quality or state of being consciously purposefully aware of something.

Proverbs 15:18 ESV

A hot-tempered man stirs up strife, but he who is slow to anger quiets contention.

Suggested Common Language Meaning

Mindfulness is calm, easy, at ease, chosen control in the moment.

*Notes:*_____
_____
_____
_____
_____
_____
_____
_____
_____

Mindfulness

Mindfulness is the skillful mental state of focused awareness on the present moment, while nonjudgmentally, calmly acknowledging and accepting emotions, feelings, thoughts, and bodily sensations; the quality or state of being consciously purposefully aware of something.

Proverbs 12:16 ESV

The vexation of a fool is known at once, but the prudent ignores an insult.

Suggested Common Language Meaning

Mindfulness allows us to remember to be skillful.

*Notes:*_____

_____
_____
_____
_____
_____
_____

Mindfulness

Mindfulness is the skillful mental state of focused awareness on the present moment, while nonjudgmentally, calmly acknowledging and accepting emotions, feelings, thoughts, and bodily sensations; the quality or state of being consciously purposefully aware of something.

James 1:5

Do any of you need wisdom? Ask God for it. He is generous and enjoys giving to everyone. So he will give you wisdom.

Suggested Common Language Meaning

Mindfulness allows us to quiet our minds and hear guidance from above.

Notes: _____

_____

_____

_____

_____

_____

_____

_____

Mindfulness

Mindfulness is the skillful mental state of focused awareness on the present moment, while nonjudgmentally, calmly acknowledging and accepting emotions, feelings, thoughts, and bodily sensations; the quality or state of being consciously purposefully aware of something.

James 3:17 ESV

But the wisdom from above is first pure, then peaceable, gentle, open to reason, full of mercy and good fruits, impartial and sincere.

Suggested Common Language Meaning

Mindfulness allows us to quiet our minds and hear guidance from above, and grows as we practice. First peaceful, relaxing, enabling wisdom, and fruits of the spirit.

Notes:_____
_____
_____
_____
_____

Mindfulness

Mindfulness is the skillful mental state of focused awareness on the present moment, while nonjudgmentally, calmly acknowledging and accepting emotions, feelings, thoughts, and bodily sensations; the quality or state of being consciously purposefully aware of something.

James 1:5 ESV

If any of you lacks wisdom, let him ask God, who gives generously to all without reproach, and it will be given him.

Suggested Common Language Meaning

Mindfulness allows us to know the wisdom of the spirit, ask and listen for guidance.

*Notes:*_____
_____
_____
_____
_____
_____
_____

Mindfulness

Mindfulness is the skillful mental state of focused awareness on the present moment, while nonjudgmentally, calmly acknowledging and accepting emotions, feelings, thoughts, and bodily sensations; the quality or state of being consciously purposefully aware of something.

Ephesians 4:29 ESV

Let no corrupting talk come out of your mouths, but only such as is good for building up, as fits the occasion, that it may give grace to those who hear.

Suggested Common Language Meaning

Mindfulness allows us to more effectively control our behavior by slowing down our thought processes and increasing purposefulness.

Notes:_____
_____
_____
_____

Mindfulness

Mindfulness is the skillful mental state of focused awareness on the present moment, while nonjudgmentally, calmly acknowledging and accepting emotions, feelings, thoughts, and bodily sensations; the quality or state of being consciously purposefully aware of something.

Proverbs 17:27 ESV

Whoever restrains his words has knowledge, and he who has a cool spirit is a man of understanding.

Suggested Common Language Meaning

Mindfulness is cool and restrained words. Allow us to be upright and understanding.

*Notes:*_____
_____
_____
_____
_____
_____
_____
_____

N

Nonjudgmental Stance

Nonjudgmental Stance is the skillful mental state of focused awareness in nonjudgment.

2 Kings 13:23 NKJV

But the Lord was gracious to them, had compassion on them, and regarded them, because of His covenant with Abraham, Isaac, and Jacob, and would not yet destroy them or cast them from His presence.

Suggested Common Language Meaning

Nonjudgmental Stance in practice is compassionate and based in Biblical covenant.

Notes:_____
_____
_____
_____
_____
_____
_____

Nonjudgmental Stance

Nonjudgmental Stance is the skillful mental state of focused awareness in nonjudgment.

Psalm 78:38 NKJV

But He, being full of compassion,
forgave their iniquity, And did not destroy them. Yes, many a time He turned His anger away, and did not stir up all His wrath;

Suggested Common Language Meaning

Nonjudgmental Stance in practice is compassionate and acknowledges the perfect in perfection that we have as human beings.

Notes:_____
_____
_____
_____
_____
_____
_____
_____

Nonjudgmental Stance

Nonjudgmental Stance is the skillful mental state of focused awareness in nonjudgment.

1 Corinthians 4:3-5 NIV

I care very little if I am judged by you or by any human court; indeed, I do not even judge myself. My conscience is clear, but that does not make me innocent. It is the Lord who judges me. Therefore judge nothing before the appointed time; wait until the Lord comes. He will bring to light what is hidden in darkness and will expose the motives of the heart. At that time each will receive their praise from God.

Suggested Common Language Meaning

I do not even judge myself. It is the Lord who judges me.

*Notes:*_____
_____
_____
_____
_____
_____

Nonjudgmental Stance

Nonjudgmental Stance is the skillful mental state of focused awareness in nonjudgment.

1 Corinthians 12:6-8 NLV

There are different ways of doing His work. But it is the same God who uses all these ways in all people. The Holy Spirit works in each person in one way or another for the good of all. One person is given the gift of teaching words of wisdom. Another person is given the gift of teaching what he has learned and knows. These gifts are by the same Holy Spirit.

Suggested Common Language Meaning

Nonjudgmental Stance is the skill of allowing, without judgment or fault finding. God uses all ways and these gifts are gifts of the spirit, to each person, in his or her own way.

*Notes:*_____
_____
_____
_____
_____

Nonjudgmental Stance

Nonjudgmental Stance is the skillful mental state of focused awareness in nonjudgment.

Romans 14:1-23 ESV

As for the one who is weak in faith, welcome him, but not to quarrel over opinions. One person believes he may eat anything, while the weak person eats only vegetables. Let not the one who eats despise the one who abstains, and let not the one who abstains pass judgment on the one who eats, for God has welcomed him. Who are you to pass judgment on the servant of another? It is before his own master that he stands or falls. And he will be upheld, for the Lord is able to make him stand. One person esteems one day as better than another, while another esteems all days alike. Each one should be fully convinced in his own mind.

Suggested Common Language Meaning

Nonjudgmental Stance is not quarreling over opinions, not despising, not passing judgment. Who are we to pass judgment upon another?

*Notes:*_____

_____

Nonjudgmental Stance

Nonjudgmental Stance is the skillful mental state of focused awareness in nonjudgment.

John 3:16-17 ESV

For God so loved the world, that he gave his only Son, that whoever believes in him should not perish but have eternal life. For God did not send his Son into the world to condemn the world, but in order that the world might be saved through him.

Suggested Common Language Meaning

Nonjudgmental Stance is to not condemn. Be Christ-like do not condemn.

Notes:_____

_____
_____
_____
_____
_____
_____
_____
_____

Nonjudgmental Stance

Nonjudgmental Stance is the skillful mental state of focused awareness in nonjudgment.

Romans 3:23 ESV

For all have sinned and fall short of the glory of God.

Suggested Common Language Meaning

All, meaning all, ourselves and others. Nonjudgmental stance must include the self and others, to be complete.

*Notes:*_____
_____
_____
_____
_____
_____
_____
_____
_____

o

One-mindfully

One-mindfully is the skillful mental state of focused awareness.

Philippians 2:2 ESV

Complete my joy by being of the same mind, having the same love, being in full accord and of one mind.

Suggested Common Language Meaning

Living within one's beliefs gives peace of mind.

*Notes:*_____

_____
_____
_____
_____
_____
_____
_____
_____
_____
_____

Pain

Pain internal subjective experience of discomfort, disease, or distress.

2 Corinthians 12:9 NKJV

And He said to me, "My grace is sufficient for you, for my strength is made perfect in weakness." Therefore most gladly I will rather boast in my infirmities, that the power of Christ may rest upon me. Therefore I take pleasure in infirmities, in reproaches, in needs, in persecutions, in distresses, for Christ's sake. For when I am weak, then I am strong.

Suggested Common Language Meaning

Remember that when we are in pain, distress, dis-ease, discomfort, distress, that Christ promised strength and grace as assistance to us.

*Notes:*_____
_____
_____
_____
_____
_____
_____

Present Moment Mindfulness

Present moment mindfulness of each new moment as it arises.

Matthew 6:34 NLV

Do not worry about tomorrow. Tomorrow will have its own worries. The troubles we have in a day are enough for one day.

Suggested Common Language Meaning

Deal with today, today and deal with tomorrow, tomorrow.

Notes:_____
_____
_____
_____
_____
_____
_____
_____
_____

R

Reasonable mind

Reasonable mind is the reason, cool, calculated part of the Wise Mind.

Isaiah 1:18-20 NKJV

"Come now, and let us reason together," Says the Lord, "Though your sins are like scarlet, they shall be as white as snow; though they are red like crimson, they shall be as wool. If you are willing and obedient, you shall eat the good of the land;

Suggested Common Language Meaning

Willingness and faith are valid reason for those desiring to be more Christ-like.

*Notes:*_____

_____
_____
_____
_____
_____
_____
_____
_____

Rest

Rest means to take a break when you are tired.

Matthew 11:28 ESV

Come to me, all who labor and are heavy laden, and I will give you rest.

Suggested Common Language Meaning

Rest in the assurances of Lords promises.

Notes:_____
_____
_____
_____
_____
_____
_____
_____
_____

S

Self-Care

Self-care is care of one's own needs.

1 Corinthians 6:19 ESV

Or do you not know that your body is a temple of the Holy Spirit within you, whom you have from God? You are not your own.

Suggested Common Language Meaning

Love yourself the way the Holy Spirit loves you. Be sure that you are on your list.

*Notes:*_____
_____
_____
_____
_____
_____
_____
_____

Sooth the Moment

Sooth the moment is the skillful addressing of the moment, when the moment is challenging and unchangeable.

Romans 8:28 ESV

And we know that for those who love God all things work together for good, for those who are called according to his purpose.

Suggested Common Language Meaning

Sooth yourself with the knowing that all things work together for good, for you.

*Notes:*_____
_____
_____
_____
_____
_____
_____
_____

Sooth the Moment

Sooth the moment is the skillful addressing of the moment, when the moment is challenging and unchangeable.

Philippians 4:19 ESV

And my God will supply every need of yours according to his riches in glory in Christ Jesus.

Suggested Common Language Meaning

Sooth yourself with the knowing that God will supply all of your needs.

*Notes:*_____

_____
_____
_____
_____
_____
_____
_____
_____

Sooth the Moment

Sooth the moment is the skillful addressing of the moment, when the moment is challenging and unchangeable.

Psalm 119:105 ESV

Your word is a lamp to my feet and a light to my path.

Suggested Common Language Meaning

Sooth yourself with the absolute knowing that God will light your way.

*Notes:*_____

_____

_____

_____

_____

_____

_____

_____

_____

Self-regulation

Self-regulation is the skill of controlling yourself and making mindful choices.

Proverbs 25:28 ESV

A man without self-control is like a city broken into and left without walls.

Suggested Common Language Meaning

Self-control is a fortress of strength. It allows us to choose our reactions rather than be tossed about on rough seas.

*Notes:*_____
_____
_____
_____
_____
_____
_____
_____
_____

Self-regulation

Self-regulation is the skill of controlling yourself and making mindful choices.

Proverbs 25:28 ESV

A man without self-control is like a city broken into and left without walls.

Suggested Common Language Meaning

Self-control is a fortress of strength. It allows us to choose our reactions rather than be tossed about on rough seas.

*Notes:*_____

_____
_____
_____
_____
_____
_____
_____

References

ESV	The Holy Bible, English Standard Version	Scripture quotations are from The ESV® Bible (The Holy Bible, English Standard Version®), copyright © 2001 by Crossway, a publishing ministry of Good News Publishers. Used by permission. All rights reserved.
ESV	Holy Bible, English Standard Version	Scripture quotations are from the ESV® Bible (The Holy Bible, English Standard Version®), copyright © 2001 by Crossway Bibles, a publishing ministry of Good News Publishers. Used by permission. All rights reserved.
EXB	Holy Bible, The Expanded Bible	Scripture taken from The Expanded Bible. Copyright ©2011 by Thomas Nelson. Used by permission. All rights reserved.

Houts, L. H., (2020). CBT - DBT Companion for Everyday Practice. Amazon Digital Services LLC - KDP Print US.

ICB	Holy Bible, International Children's Bible	Scripture taken from the International Children's Bible®. Copyright © 1986, 1988, 1999 by Thomas Nelson. Used by permission. All rights reserved.

Linehan, M. (1993). Cognitive-behavioral treatment of borderline personality disorder. Guilford Press.

Linehan, M. (n.d.). DBT Skills training manual (1st ed.). Guilford Publications.

Linehan, M. M. (2014). DBT skills training handouts and worksheets (2nd ed.). Guilford Publications.

NCV	Holy Bible, New	Scripture taken from the New Century

	Century Version	Version®. Copyright © 2005 by Thomas Nelson. Used by permission. All rights reserved.
NET	Holy Bible, New English Translation	Scripture quoted by permission. Quotations designated New English Translation (NET) are from the NET Bible® copyright ©1996, 2019 by Biblical Studies Press, L.L.C. http://netbible.com All rights reserved.
NIV	Holy Bible, New International Version	New International Version and NIV® (collectively, "NIV") are registered trademarks of Biblica in the United States and other countries. All rights reserved.
NKJV	Holy Bible, New King James Version	Scripture taken from the New King James Version®. Copyright © 1982 by Thomas Nelson. Used by permission. All rights reserved.
NLV	Holy Bible, *New Life Version*	Scripture quotations are taken from the *New Life Version*, copyright © 1969 and 2003. Used by permission of Barbour Publishing, Inc., Uhrichsville, Ohio 44683. All rights reserved.

Made in the USA
Middletown, DE
10 April 2025

74084480R00117